LEGALLY CLUELESS

CLUELESS

A Law Guide for the Rest of Us

Eric Schnapp

Denise Schnapp

William Schnapp

Legally Clueless: A law guide for the rest of us.

Second edition
© 2003 by Eric, Denise, and William Schnapp

ISBN: 0-9719337-7-4
Library of Congress Control Number: 2003090516

Printed and bound in the United States of America
Published by Colletes & Sons
An imprint of Elma Colletes & Sons
5895 Garden Reach Cove, Memphis, TN, 38120

Dedicated to our grandparents:

Manoel and Elza
and
Isak and Martha

(...and of course, to our parents, Moacir and Elma, who threatened to disown us if their names were not mentioned in the book!!)

Disclaimer!

*"A defendant is entitled to a fair trial,
but not a perfect one."*

U.S. Supreme Court

This book is intended only as a guide, not as legal advice. Each case is different; every state, county, and city has its own little peculiarities, so don't expect a basic, general guide like this one to be a substitute for a lawyer. Use this book as a learning aid only. Besides, who would trust their legal problems to three youngsters like us?

When in trouble, get legal counsel. Despite all the jokes about attorneys and their somewhat undeserved reputation, there is nothing more comforting than a good lawyer holding your hand when you are facing a judge in court. The American judicial system may be flawed, but there is none better.

Table of Contents

Traffic Law 13

Crimes 35

Drugs and Alcohol 43

Sex, Rape,and Harassment 51

Credit, Bad Credit, and Bankruptcy 55

Renting a Home 61

College 67

Wills, Trusts, and Power of Attorney 69

Small Claims, Mediation, and Arbitration 75

Jobs 81

Traveling Abroad 89

Citizenship 95

Computers, the Internet, and You 105

Index 117

Introduction

"Nothing is to be preferred before justice."

-Socrates

Whether you realize it or not, you are constantly either following the laws or breaking them. Every time you stop at a red light you are obeying the law. When you pay your bills or your taxes on time, when you trim the tree branches that are about to fall on a neighbor's car, or when a simple "no" stops your sexual advances, you are accepting and complying with previously established rules that facilitate life in our society. These rules level out the playing field for most of us. The law protects you, your family, and your property against people who are stronger, greedier, or just meaner than you are. That means that you can't take a little kid's ice cream, nor are you entitled to shoplift at Wal-Mart just because they make more money than you do.

The idea for this book came one day when I was pulled over for speeding. While the blue lights were flashing behind my car, I realized then that despite all my years in school I didn't really know anything about the law, or how to deal with this situation. What do I do now? What if I forgot my license and registration? Could I be arrested if I was driving twenty miles above the speed limit? What if he wants me to take a breathalyzer? What if the breathalyzer mistakenly shows I've been drinking? What about next year's insurance premiums? Is my dad gonna kill me?

After the officer kindly let me go with just a warning, I went searching for a book about my rights and obligations as they pertained to the law, but I didn't find anything useful at my level. What I found was either too basic or too sophisticated.

After talking with my sister Denise, a sophomore at Vanderbilt in Nashville, and my brother William, a junior at Emory in Atlanta, we realized that I was not alone in my ignorance. We decided then to research and write a book about the law for people like us; those young and unprepared for life and bored stiff reading text without pictures. We tried to make the book as interesting and vibrant as possible while retaining the seriousness of the subject, devoting attention to legal obligations and rights. If sometimes we sound too blunt or uncaring, it's because we don't want the book to read as being judgmental or patronizing.

We hope you will enjoy this book more than we did writing it. The work was much harder than we had anticipated, and we missed our summer altogether. Worst of all, our friends are now justified in calling us geeks.

Eric Schnapp

"It may be true that the law cannot make a man love me, but it can keep him from lynching me, and I think that's pretty important".

Dr. Martin Luther King, Jr.

CHAPTER ONE

Traffic Law

"Men have feelings, but the law does not"
-Napoleon I

Rites of passage vary from culture to culture, ranging from bungee jumping into a mud pit with a vine tied to one's ankles to a Jewish Bar Mitzvah. In American culture there is no more important or joyous event than "The Driver's License" and, strangely enough, it coincides with the ubiquitous, "I Can't Wait To Move Out Of Here" phenomenon. A driver's license and a car mean freedom to come and go as one pleases, but this most awaited event comes with its own price tag: rules. You can't really come and go as you please, otherwise you may be slapped with the dreaded *ticket* (or worse). Tickets should be avoided like the plague unless you don't mind risking the loss of your driving privileges. Sooner or later, though, everyone makes a few mistakes and gets caught in the act.

Traffic violations come in two flavors: non-moving and, you guessed it, moving.
- Speeding,
- Running a red light
- Illegal passing
- Illegal turn
- Disrespecting a railroad sign
- Driving under the influence
- Driving without a license

These are just some of the moving violations that can cost you money, points on your driver's license, a court appearance, and even time in jail.

Non-moving violations are mostly related to illegal parking, but an expired tag can also get you. While these fines are usually less expensive, they may still lead to a court appearance but no points will be counted against on your license.

Your driver's license is issued by the state where you reside and when you move to another state, generally, you should apply for a new license within thirty days. It is not necessary to change it if you're just going to an out-of-state school and keeping your primary residence.

Remember that all correspondence regarding traffic violations will be mailed to the address on your driver's license, and if your parents live there, they may see the ticket before you do. If you fail to check your mail for long periods of time, a ticket could inadvertently go unpaid and may lead to harsher penalties from traffic courts including the possibility of an arrest warrant being issued against you.

Before crossing state lines, a young driver should check the driving age requirement of the state to be visited. A state that requires drivers to be seventeen or older, for example, may not honor the license of a sixteen-year-old motorist.

"Pull over!"

What should I do if I'm pulled over?
Don't panic (even if you have a reason to). Slow down and calmly find a safe spot to park the vehicle. Stay in the car.

What if it is not my car the cops are after?
If you are not sure it is your vehicle the squad car is after, start to pull over and it will pass you by if you are not the intended target.

What if the blue lights are not from a real squad car?
This is an unusual occurrence, but sexual predators have been known to use fake police lights to prey on their victims. If you fear that the blue lights following you are not from a legitimate police car, decrease your speed, turn on your blinker to acknowledge your intention to stop, and drive to a safe, well lit, or populated area. A real officer may not like having to follow you for a couple of miles, but they'll usually understand.

What should I do after I stop?
Don't rush to grab your license. Instead, turn off the engine. Keep your hands on the steering wheel, and wait for instructions. Cops will carefully approach you from the rear since they have no way of telling whether you are a desperate criminal or a law-abiding citizen. If they become suspicious, you may end up with a stressed, and irritated armed cop. Not the best scenario for trying to talk yourself out of a ticket.

Don't remove your seatbelt after being pulled over. The officer may assume you were not using one and he or she may slap you with another charge.

The officer will ask for your license and registration which you should calmly produce and again place your hands on the wheel. Most of the time only routine questions will be asked. If you feel that any of your responses could somehow be incriminating, instead of lying to a law enforcement officer, you may just refuse to answer them. No reason is necessary but you can always state you don't feel comfortable being questioned without the presence of an attorney.

The cop will then return to the patrol car to check the truth of the information you provided as well as to look for outstanding tickets or warrants against you. This will take a few minutes. Just wait for the officer to return. If later, a ticket is indeed issued to you, the officer will recite the standard routine regarding the traffic infraction. In many states you will have to sign the ticket to acknowledge receiving it. Lack of either could possibly result in the ticket being dismissed later on. Signing the ticket is not an admission of guilt. Failure to sign it, however, could result in you being taken into custody, since a ticket is issued as a substitute for an arrest.

When the cop allows you to go (remember to leave only after you're told to do so), don't show your frustration by "peeling off." It could be considered reckless driving, and it may get you another ticket or even arrested. Also, it is not unusual for a motorist who just got a ticket to curse, even if it is to oneself. Depending on the mood of the officer, it can change a simple traffic violation into an arrest for disorderly conduct.

What if the officer asks me if I know why I was pulled over?
From the moment a driver is stopped, anything the motorist says or does can be used in a court of law, so don't be cute! Do not argue and be sure to address the officer as sir or ma'am. Do not volunteer

any information, and don't apologize for what you think you may have done since it could be construed as admission of guilt. If asked whether you know why you have been stopped, "no" should be your answer; the officer may have pulled you over for an infraction other than what you think you may have committed.

What if I just forgot my license at home?

If caught driving without a valid license on your person, you can be ticketed and may have to appear in court. If the driver can later demonstrate that he or she had a valid license at the time of the infraction, the charges could be dropped. Still, be prepared to pay the usual court costs.

You may improve things a bit by memorizing your driver's license number, or better yet, by keeping a photocopy of your license in the glove compartment.

What if I'm caught with an expired license?

You will at least get a ticket. Depending on the reason you were stopped, an expired license can be added as an aggravating factor,such as, an accident with injured people.

What if my license was suspended or revoked?

Now you're in trouble. Driving with a revoked or suspended driver's license is a more serious offense, and it will likely get the driver arrested on the spot. It can possibly even lead to jail time depending on the original reason for the loss of the license.

Speed detection methods

The police may stop a driver for speeding, but unless there is objective verification of the actual speed, no ticket can be issued. Several ways to measure speed can be used.

Pacing: The driver of the squad car matches the speed of his or her vehicle with yours. This method is definitely low-tech but effective. The squad car's speedometer has to be calibrated since the error in a factory-installed speedometer is considerable. In court, a defendant may request the calibration records for the police car's speedometer. Failure to produce those records can result in the ticket being dismissed.

Radar: A radar emits radio waves that are bounced off your car then back to the radar device. The waves change pitch depending on the speed of the moving vehicle, like the whistle of a passing train, and that change in pitch is read as the vehicle speed. Radar detectors are usually very effective, but it is difficult to single out one car from a group. The radar is also sensitive to interference. The device must be calibrated with a special tuning fork and, if the ticket is challenged in court, the patrolman has to present calibration records for the radar's accuracy.

Laser: This device uses invisible light waves bounced off your car. It can only work in a direct line-of-sight, but it can pick out a car among many. By the time your onboard laser detector sounds the alarm, the vehicle will probably have already been clocked. Same as above, lasers must be calibrated and appropriate records kept.

Average speed: By measuring the time it takes for a car to go from point A to point B, a known distance, an officer can easily measure the average speed of a vehicle. It is a simple but very effective method. Any good stopwatch will suffice, without the need for fancy gadgets or special calibration.

Searches

Can the cops "frisk" me?

Yes. If probable cause exists, a routine patting over the clothes searching for weapons is not improper. A more thorough body search may be necessary when looking for drugs and it is not unusual for a person who is being searched to feel harassed.

Do the cops have the right to search my car?

The driving rights of a citizen are firmly established by the U.S. Constitution, and being pulled over doesn't change that. The Fourth Amendment protects a vehicle (as well as one's domicile) against unreasonable searches. No legal search can occur without a warrant unless the officer observes something suspicious, such as a driver who reaches under the seat of his car, or when unlawful items are in plain view of the police, (such as empty beer cans on the floor of the vehicle, or drug paraphernalia). This may provide legal grounds to do a search, and the officer's testimony, as well as the items found during that search, will generally be admissible in court.

What if the officer searches my car without a reason?

Any criminal evidence discovered by the police through an illegal or unreasonable search may not be used against you during a trial. However, if your attorney fails to persuade the court that the evidence was unlawfully obtained, it may still be used against you.

What if the police ask my permission to search the car?

A warrant is not necessary when a driver (or a homeowner) gives permission for a police search. Remember, if no probable cause exists, the police officer has to ask the driver whether he or she will allow the vehicle to be searched.

Even hardened criminals, stopped for traffic violations while transporting illegal drugs in their vehicles, have been videotaped giving officers permission to search their car. Never underestimate the pressure exerted by an authority figure. If no good reason exists to permit the officer to search your vehicle, politely decline it.

What if the car is impounded. Can they search it?
If an infraction or accident requires that a vehicle be towed, the police officer is required to make an itemized list of the contents in the car to insure their proper return to the owner. If suspicious items are found during this process, the cops may then have probable cause to search the vehicle further, sometimes even taking it apart, piece-by-piece.

Americans driving in Canada

A license tag from a southern state is alleged to be an invitation for Canadian officers to stop and search that vehicle. This may be due to the belief that cars driven by Southerners are more likely to carry weapons.

Even if you don't own a gun, the discovery of a single round of ammunition in your car may get you in trouble with the Canadian police.

Arrests

What if the cop tells me I'm under arrest?
If you are placed under arrest do not argue and do not resist. The officer has been trained to rapidly increase force in response to any threat or resistance, real or perceived, and you may end up seriously hurt and also charged with resisting arrest.

What if I'm not guilty?
Tough luck. When placing you under arrest, the cop has already decided that a cause for your arrest exists, and no amount of pleading or crying is likely to stop the process. You'll have to wait and argue your case in court. If you are proven not guilty, the charges of resisting arrest may be dismissed, unless the courts decide it is a separate offense.

Save your "fight" for a courtroom and you may win. Fight in the street with an officer, and you will always lose.

What if they don't read me my rights?
The cops don't have to read you your rights during the arrest process unless they are trying to obtain a confession from you. This means that if you volunteer self-incriminating information to the cops, without being asked by them, it could be used against you even if you have not been explained your rights. Keep your mouth shut.

An officer is bound by law to read one's rights only after the person is put in police custody. Therefore, the"innocent chat" with the patrolman while he's writing you a ticket can be used against you. The famous "Miranda Law" simply states that a confession is not admissible in court unless the person's rights have been explained, that is:

- The right to remain silent
- The right to have an attorney present during questioning
- The right against self-incrimination

Do they have to use handcuffs?

Dangerous criminal or not, this is standard procedure. The officer will ask you to place your hands behind your back. If you refuse, the cops have been trained to force you into submission, and it is not unusual for a wrist sprain or a fracture to occur. It is healthier to cooperate.

Where will they take me?

You will normally be placed in a holding cell with scores of other people who are meaner and dirtier than you are. Nothing in that cell separates college students from hardened criminals.

Tickets

Can I talk myself out of a ticket?
It is difficult but you can always try. Flirting or slightly pulling up your skirt for a male officer will very likely get you nowhere (not even if you are a girl).

If you've never had a ticket for a moving violation, say so. Even hardened cops may not like to break a lucky streak. You are, however, more likely to succeed if you can convince the officer that paying the ticket and the likely increase in insurance premium will be a major financial burden. Works best if you are indeed poor and driving a beat-up car. If it is your birthday month, or better yet, the very day, ask for sympathy.

Bribery may work in certain parts of the world but in the U.S. it is not only a serious crime but will strongly offend the majority of officers. Don't even think about it!

What is the *point system*? Can it cost me my license?
Each state has its own version of the point system. Each type of moving violation is assigned a certain number of points depending on the seriousness of the infraction. Significant violations correspond to more points, and a driver's license may be suspended or revoked if enough points are attained within a defined period of time.

A license is considered a privilege and can be suspended or revoked for a single violation, such as driving under the influence, reckless driving, speeding, refusing a sobriety test, or leaving the scene of an accident. Multiple minor infractions, including the parking tickets you've ignored, can lead to the same results.

What happens to my insurance premiums?

An occasional ticket such as a single speeding violation in three years is unlikely to raise your premiums. The insurance companies look for repeat offenders who are more likely to suffer accidents, and these drivers may be penalized with higher rates or outright cancellation of the insurance. These companies have access to the Department of Motor Vehicles (DMV) records, and they may also use their own point system to judge a customer's insurance worthiness.

Depending on the frequency and seriosness of traffic violations incurred by an individual, the insurance company may assess increased premiums and points for the whole family, if a single policy covers them all. They can go as far as to cancel the coverage for the entire family.

What options do I have after receiving a ticket?

A) You may decide to pay the ticket by mail or in person, implicitly admitting guilt. You will be assessed the corresponding points on your driver's license and your insurance premiums may increase.

B) If you feel there's a solid defense, you may plead "not guilty" and go to trial.

C) You may plead *no contest*. This may allow you to pay the fine or attend traffic school without admitting guilt.

D) You forget about the ticket or decide not to pay it. A warrant will probably be issued for your arrest.

When in court, if a judge asks you whether you would like to have a ticket dismissed in exchange for court costs, take it! You have been given an "out" and if you insist on fighting the ticket you better have a great defense because the judge is likely to rule against you.

Is traffic school an option?

Depending on the state, you may be offered the option to attend a defensive driving school. This is, provided that you have not done so in the previous 12 months and you agree not to challenge the ticket. Opting for driving school usually implies admission of guilt.

Traffic school is a bargain. Usually two four-hour sessions must be attended, but even if you have to pay the fine, tickets may not go on your record, no points will be assessed, and consequently no insurance premium increases are likely. You may want to save your "Get Out of Jail Free" card for one of the more serious violations.

How long will the ticket stay on my insurance record?

Most companies keep the traffic violation points for three to five years but DUIs may remain on your records substantially longer. If no new violations occur during that time, your points may be reduced.

When do I need an attorney?

You should only consider representing yourself in court in cases of non-moving violations or simple moving violations, such as going five miles above the speed limit. When stakes are high, it is best to seek legal counsel since lawyers understand the intricacies of the judicial system and can best make use of the "wheeling and dealing" that occurs in everyday court proceedings.

You should seek legal counsel every time you are charged with a more serious violation, such as DUI or when personal injury or significant property damage exists. If you are not sure whether you need full representation from a lawyer, you can always obtain a one time consultation from an attorney.

What happens in traffic court?

A trial before the judge occurs when you plead "not guilty". A court date is set so both you and the officer who gave you the ticket can be present. Remember that you always have the right to face your accuser.

If you don't appear, a warrant may be issued for your arrest. If the officer doesn't show up, the ticket may be dismissed.

Your case will be heard in a room full of other people accused of traffic violations. When your name is called, you'll step forward to face the judge and the ticketing officer who will first give his or her version of the facts to the judge. You have the right to examine any evidence introduced by the police, and you can question the officer. Afterwards, you will be allowed to present your own view of the facts to the judge, including any witnesses you brought to testify on your behalf. The judge will then promptly come up with a decision. The whole process is rather dry, quick, and matter-of-fact, unlike the movies.

What if I get an out-of state ticket?

In the past, many drivers would disregard an out-of-state fine, assuming that the ticket would not reach their state's DMV. Now most states exchange information regarding tickets, and if they go unpaid, your driver's license could be suspended. Remember that any notice regarding a suspended license will be mailed to your address of record. Check your mail.

Obsolete DMV computers have been known to suspend or revoke a driver's license for an out-of-state infraction, and simply fail to send the motorist any notification. Your first clue that you've been driving without a valid license may conceivably come when a police officer arrests you, after checking your license on a routine traffic violation.

DUI

DUI refers to "driving under the influence" of alcohol or drugs. It has been estimated that around fifty percent of all fatal traffic accidents are related to DUI, therefore, the law is particularly sensitive to this subject. Even a glass of wine at dinner may impair your ability to drive, and larger amounts certainly will do so. The higher the blood alcohol level, the more impaired a person's reflexes will be, and an experienced cop can easily estimate the amount of alcohol consumed just based on the driver's behavior.

What if I just drank beer?
The widespread belief that drinking beer is less intoxicating than hard liquor is a common error. Even though the alcohol concentration is different in each beverage, the amount of alcohol in a glass of wine, a can of beer, or a shot of whiskey is approximately the same. The blood alcohol level depends both on the amount and the speed of alcohol consumption, as well as, the stomach's contents. A large meal will slow down the alcohol absorption.

Note that since it takes a while for any ingested alcohol to reach your circulation, that "last round" at the bar may increase your blood alcohol level just as you're driving back home.

How much alcohol does it take to be considered DUI?
In most states a driver with an alcohol concentration of 0.08 or higher may be charged with DUI. Lower blood levels can also lead to DUI charges if the motorist exhibits obvious signs of intoxication, such as erratic driving, swerving, or decreased motor coordination.

Under lab conditions, it takes an average adult male four drinks ingested on an empty stomach in the period of one hour to reach a BAC of 0.08 or greater. It would take an average female only three drinks to reach that same level, due to a woman's smaller body mass. Most drivers will show a substantial decrease in their driving abilities even at a much smaller BAC.

What about prescription medications and illegal drugs?

A motorist can be charged with driving under the influence even if only over-the-counter or prescription drugs have been ingested. It is the driver's responsibility to read the warnings on the medicine label regarding driving as well as the operation of heavy machinery, and to refrain from doing so if impaired.

Sedating antihistamines, for example, may decrease one's driving abilities just as much as illegal drugs or alcohol. Driving home after having a surgical or dental procedure during which sedatives have been administered can result in a DUI.

If there is evidence of illegal drug use in a DUI case, it may bring additional charges and penalties, such as mandatory jail time.

How can the cops tell I've been drinking?

Sobriety tests can be done simply by evaluating the motorist's coordination, like asking the driver to touch the tip of his or her nose with eyes closed, walking a straight line, or standing up with feet close together for a few seconds. An experienced cop can judge the alcohol level just by listening to the typically slurred speech of an intoxicated driver. Many other substances besides alcohol can lead to a similar lack of coordination.

The eyes are often a dead giveaway in cases of alcohol intoxication. Gazing to either side while holding the head still causes the eyes to oscillate rapidly (like a hyperactive pendulum) and the intensity of this oscillation depends on the blood alcohol level. Based on this and other tests, if the officer believes you are intoxicated, you may be asked to take an alcohol breath test.

What is a "breathalyzer"?

Can't you tell when someone has been drinking just by the smell of alcohol? So can the breathalyzer, a device that can determine the blood alcohol level by analyzing one's breath. The amount of alcohol exhaled by the lungs (not the mouth) is proportional to the alcohol concentration in the blood. A simple handheld unit is often used to test drivers, but a more accurate instrument may be present in the squad car, or in a separate DUI vehicle.

Can I demand a blood test instead of the breathalyzer?

Some states allow the driver to choose between a breath, blood, and urine test. A sober driver may well prefer a blood test, since it is more precise and a second sample may be drawn and kept in the lab, just in case the first sample yields questionable results. Remember, however, that blood and urine samples can and routinely are tested for several substances other than alcohol. The breathalyzer detector is sensitive only to alcohol!

If your state does not allow you to choose a more precise alcohol test, it may be wise to use your cell phone to call your attorney and ask for help. A lawyer may pull some strings to demand a blood and/or urine sample for further independent testing.

What if the breathalyzer says I am intoxicated?

You may be charged with DUI, but in many states your driver's license can be suspended even if they decide not to prosecute.

What if I refuse a sobriety test?

Failure to submit to a sobriety test can result in automatic license suspension for up to one year and other penalties, even if the driver has not been drinking! If you refuse a sobriety test, it considerably increases the likelihood that a judge or a jury will give more weight to the police testimony regarding the intoxicated appearance of the driver. An officer must inform the driver of his or her rights before any testing for intoxication is done.

Are my rights being violated when the cops test me?

Because alcohol is eliminated from the body in a matter of hours, in most states the courts allow the officer to test your sobriety on the spot, without the presence of an attorney. However, there must be reasonable suspicion for the cops to stop a driver, such as erratic driving, swerving on the road, speeding, or even throwing a beer can out of the car.

Can I hide the smell of alcohol with mouthwash?

Good try but no, you can't. Trying to conceal the alcohol odor by quickly rinsing with mouthwash may backfire since many of these products actually contain alcohol. The breathalyzer can't distinguish between the alcohol present in your mouth from that which is exhaled by the lungs.

Most states require that twenty minutes or so elapse before administering a breathalyzer test. This allows time for recently ingested alcohol to dissipate from the mouth, thus avoiding measuring anything other than the alcohol exhaled by the lungs.

What if they see an empty beer can in my car?

Even states that have delayed enacting an open container law are now rushing to do it, or they risk losing federal funds. If an open container is found, in most states you may not only be ticketed and subjected to sobriety tests, but your vehicle can, as a consequence, be legally scarched.

What if I'm under 21 and I had only one drink?

Most states agree in setting the alcohol limit close to zero for drivers under 21, meaning no tolerance for any amount of alcohol. Remember that refusal to take a sobriety test may result in a minimum one-year suspension of your driver's license, whether you've been drinking or not.

What are the penalties for a first time DUI?

For starters, you will be arrested and fined. In most states the driver will spend a minimum of four hours in a holding cell to "cool off", even if bail has been posted. A first time DUI can lead to license suspension, as well as, jail time, depending on the circumstances. The judge is more likely to exchange possible time in jail for community service when it relates to a first time offender.

What about repeat offenders?

Multiple DUI offenses change things dramatically. The amount of fines and the chances for mandatory time in jail increase with each offense, as do the chances that the driver's license will be revoked for years, or possibly even for life. The judge may also require that the driver participate in a drug and alcohol rehabilitation program. The presence of victims in a DUI case adds to the gravity of the offense, and in cases of fatal injuries you could be charged with homicide.

Can a person be charged for falling asleep at the wheel?

Sleep deprived motorists are, on average, as likely to cause accidents as drunk drivers. A motorist who is stopped for swerving or is involved in an accident could face additional charges, if driving while knowingly sleep deprived.

A large number of truck drivers, possibly even the majority, suffer from excessive daytime sleepiness due to, among other reasons, too many working hours. So do many college students who change their sleeping habits after moving away from home.

Auto Accidents

What do I do if I'm involved in a car accident?

First of all, stop! A simple fender-bender can become a real pain if you leave the scene of an accident, even if it was not your fault and nobody was injured.

Second, get out of harm's way, and make sure oncoming vehicles are alerted to potential road hazards created by the wreck. Use common sense deciding whether to move a vehicle or not. Call 911 if you suspect there are injured people.

Once the emergencies have been resolved, try to obtain the name and address of the other motorist, driver's license number, and insurance information. Also, get name, address, and phone numbers of any witnesses. Do not volunteer any information that could be construed as admission of guilt, but make notes if the other driver admits to distractions, such as drinking, speeding, etc. Write down any observation that may help you later, including the other driver's possible intoxicated behavior, weather conditions, speed, time of day, or unsafe state of the other vehicle.

Especially note whether people in the other car were restrained, since lack of seatbelts may increase the likelihood and severity of injuries. A jury may find that an unrestrained person may have contributed to his or her own injuries, thus possibly reducing your own liability.

Talking on the phone while driving has become an important cause of traffic accidents. Phone records can and regularly are used to prove that a motorist was on the phone while driving. An attorney may use this information to prove that the resulting distraction was in part responsible for the accident. The same may apply for mishaps involving other types of distraction such as eating, reading maps, and applying make-up.

Do I have to have car insurance?

In all states some level of insurance is mandatory, and without it, you can't lease a car or obtain a car loan. Keep proof of insurance in the vehicle or you may end up with a ticket.

Do I have to tell the insurance carrier if I have a car accident?

When contacting the insurance company, you have to do it in a "timely fashion", which usually means as soon as you are finished at the scene of the accident. It allows the insurance carrier the opportunity to research the circumstances of the crash.

If the property damage was small, you may opt not to disclose the accident to your insurance since it could increase next year's premiums more than the actual expense of repairing your vehicle. Your coverage may even be cancelled if you have multiple accidents. Don't forget, however, that the insurance company receives information about moving violations directly from the DMV, whether you report an accident to the carrier or not.

Remember also that failure to promptly notify the insurance company of an accident can result in cancellation of your policy, refusal by the company to pay for any liability, or failure to provide you with an attorney if a civil suit is brought against you.

Do I have to call the police?

Always call the police if there are victims or when substantial property damage occurred. The law in most states requires that the police should be called or at least notified, even if both parties agree to leave.

If you are at fault in a relatively small accident, you may choose to settle on the spot with the other driver by paying for the other car's damages instead of reporting the accident. Make sure to get a signed statement from the other party containing a full release from any future claims, in exchange for the sum of money you give the other motorist. Without it, you could later be sued for medical bills, lost wages, and more.

If you are not at fault, always call the police and your insurance company, even if it is a minor fender-bender. You would be amazed, once both parties leave the scene of the accident, at how quickly it can all become your fault. A few days later you could receive an unexpected call from an attorney representing the other driver, who now claims to have been injured by you. Being nice may end up being expensive.

CHAPTER TWO

Crimes

*"To my friends, everything;
to my enemies, the law."*
-Anonymous

A crime is anything that the law says it is. Laws can be passed by Congress as well as by state and local legislative bodies, and therefore they vary in different communities according to local customs. Laws are continuously being revised to accommodate changes in the structure of society and as to what constitutes accepted behavior. Over the past three decades, for example, tougher laws have been enacted against racial discrimination and drug use, while there has been a simultaneous relaxation on laws dealing with sex and homosexuality.

The intrinsic complexity of the legal system is substantially increased by the same people responsible for enforcing it. The police, judges, and lawyers are humans with their own set of values, family problems, time constraints, and financial obligations that can "color" their decisions. A prosecutor who's late for a daughter's soccer game may opt to accept a plea bargain in order to expedite the process. This is not an exaggeration, and many such examples, sometimes bordering on the absurd, happen everyday throughout the American judicial system. Furthermore, the accused's age, race, sex, and education often dictate the difference between a "slap on the wrist" and doing time in jail.

If charged with a serious crime, one needs both luck and access to a good attorney.

What is the difference between a misdemeanor and a felony?

The distinction is made based on the potential for time in jail: a crime punishable by less than one year imprisonment is considered a *misdemeanor*, while a crime that carries a possible sentence greater than one year is considered a *felony*. This definition holds even if no actual time is spent in jail.

An *infraction* is a small crime punishable by fines only, such as a traffic ticket. It does not carry the possibility of jail time. Sometimes a misdemeanor may be punishable by fines only, such as the possession of a small amount of marijuana, which is a misdemeanor but rarely leads to time in prison.

What is an accessory to the crime?

In legal terms, someone who commits a crime is called a *principal*, and any person who helps a criminal charged with a felony may be called an *accessory*. A person who was present during the actual commission of a crime, for example as a lookout or a driver during a robbery, can be charged as *principal in the second degree*. An *accessory before the fact* is an individual who helps the criminal in the planning stages but does not actually commit the crime, while an *accessory after the fact* is someone who helps the criminal afterwards, such as aiding him or her to evade capture.

What happens after the arrest?

The suspect is taken to the police station to be "booked". That means searched, photographed, and fingerprinted, and then taken to a holding cell until the first appearance in court. In the meantime, the information obtained by the police, called the arrest report, is provided to a prosecuting attorney who makes an initial decision whether to charge the accused depending on the presence of sufficient evidence. Often, a suspect's criminal record is also taken into account. A complaint with the court is then filed for one or multiple crimes. A prosecutor has a lot of latitude in deciding to bring up charges against the accused and may even choose not to prosecute a case in which an otherwise good citizen without prior criminal history has made a mistake.

What is an arraignment?

The accused, now called a defendant after being charged, is brought before the Court to be informed of these charges and of his or her rights. This is often combined with an arraignment, which is when the defendant enters a plea of guilty or not guilty. A plea of guilty is followed by a fine and/or incarceration for a time, while a plea of not guilty leads to a trial.

What is a preliminary hearing?

A preliminary hearing occurs after a defendant pleads not guilty, and it allows the court a chance to evaluate the information against the accused. It is then decided whether there is enough probable cause to proceed with a trial or send the case to the grand jury, which will or will not return an indictment.

What is a *grand jury*?

A *grand jury* consists of a group of six or more appointed citizens who decide whether a case should go to trial, based on the evidence presented by the prosecutor. If the majority of a grand jury decides in favor of prosecution, they return an indictment, which may be then followed by official charges from the District Attorney against the defendant.

What is bail?

Bail is a cash deposit posted by the defendant as a guarantee that he or she will appear in court for trial, with the money being forfeited if the accused is a no-show. A bail hearing must occur within 48 hours of the arrest. The amount of bail is set by the judge based on many factors, including the seriousness of the crime, the wealth and character of the person, and the likeliness that the defendant will not to appear in court. The defendant may, on the other hand, be released on his or her *own recognizance,* meaning that no bail is required. Serious crimes such as a first-degree murder may not allow for bail.

A bail bond is basically a promissory note one can use for a court required deposit. Bail bondsmen loans are similar to a bank's.

They charge a fee for the loan and demand some form of guarantee. If you fail to appear in court, (or jump bail), the bondsman is responsible the full amount demanded by the law. The bondsman may then foreclose on the person who pledged assets to secure the bail bond, and a bounty hunter may even track the defendant for a "friendly" visit.

When is plea bargaining an option?

The judicial system resources are strained: prosecutors have too many cases, court appointed attorneys are scarce, and a single trial may take weeks or even months. To make the cases "move", prosecutors and defense attorneys can make deals, often reducing the severity of the charges or the length of the sentence in exchange for a speedy resolution.

The vast majority of convictions result from negotiated pleas. A defendant charged with a felony may plead guilty to a reduced charge instead of risk going to trial. Plea-bargaining may be done any time *after* the arrest but *before* a verdict is reached.

Can I plead *nolo contendere*?

By pleading *nolo contendere* (Latin for "no contest") the defendant does not admit guilt but does not argue the charges either. It has the same value as a guilty plea in a criminal case and is often part of a deal offered by the prosecutor. It allows the defendant to "save face" later, and by not admitting guilt, the accused may better defend him or herself in the event of a future civil suit.

Does the jury decide the sentence?

In most states, no. The jury's only concern is whether a defendant is guilty or not. The judge does the sentencing based on statutes that address each specific crime and the maximum penalty for that particular crime. With the exception of mandatory sentencing for some types of crime, the judge has a lot of latitude in determining the punishment. A previous criminal record, unnecessary violence, and lack of remorse are all aggravating factors that are likely to generate maximum sentencing. On the other hand, a good citizen, without prior criminal history, who steals to feed or shelter his or her family is more likely to be put on probation.

What are the alternatives to jail time?

Many times the judge has the option to suspend a jail sentence and place an individual on probation. The person is to remain free as long as the conditions for the probation are met for the specified period of time. This includes periodic meetings with a probation officer, mandatory reporting of any change in address or intent to travel outside the jurisdiction, and the observance of *all laws*, not just the ones related to the crime. The judge may forbid the defendant from associating with certain individuals or frequenting certain places. Periodic drug screens are often required after the completion of a drug and alcohol rehabilitation program. If the conditions for the probation are not met, the originally suspended sentence may be reinstated in its entirety, along with punishment for any new crimes. Shoplifting a candy bar is enough of a reason to revoke probation.

Community service is an alternative punishment that is often part of probation. Lecturing to schoolchildren on the dangers of using drugs, volunteering at the hospital, and collecting trash by the roadside are just some examples.

Fines and restitution are monetary penalties set by the judge. The first is regulated and limited by law to a maximum according to the crime; the other is estimated according to the victim's loss.

One less common alternative to regular jail time is *house arrest*, in which an ankle bracelet indicating the person's whereabouts is often worn. Another alternative is *weekend jail,* which allows the individual to work and sleep at home during weekdays, but mandates the person reports back to prison on weekends.

What is the "three-strike law"?

This law states that a third conviction for a felony carries a mandatory sentence of life in prison without the possibility of parole, leaving judges no discretionary power. Although designed to serve as a deterrent to hardened criminals, it may also affect non-violent criminals. For example, one conviction for a bad check, one for a hazing episode with injury, and another conviction for possession of a couple of ounces of marijuana could theoretically put someone behind bars forever. However, recent U.S. Supreme Court decisions have required subsequent charges to be of greater severity to trigger a life sentence.

If convicted, how long does it stay on my files? Can I clean my record?

A conviction for a felony will likely remain on your records forever. A conviction as a juvenile may remain under seal of the Court when you become eighteen. An adult first convicted of certain misdemeanors may after a substantial period of time, usually several years, request that his or her records regarding the conviction be expunged, which removes it from public access allowing, however, a "for your eyes only" exception for law officers. This enables the person to truthfully deny any prior conviction when applying for a job or a license that requires a clean record. Note that a sealed record does not disappear and it will still be included as part of one's prior criminal history.

What is the difference between a civil and a criminal suit?

A criminal suit is essentially a governmental procedure. A prosecutor acting on behalf of the community, or the People, works to prove that an individual has broken the law. The prosecutor does not need permission of the victim to proceed, but, in order to win the case, he or she must prove to a jury that the defendant is guilty "beyond a reasonable doubt".

A civil suit does not involve a prosecutor because there is no crime against the People. Instead, it relies on the alleged victim (a person or an institution) to file a lawsuit against someone or an organization to seek justice and/or monetary compensation (no jail time results from civil suits). Product liability, car accidents, and patent infringement are just a few types of cases amenable to civil suits. A prosecutor is not involved in this kind of litigation, and the victim has to prove his or her case not "beyond a reasonable doubt" but only by a "preponderance of the evidence", described as more than fifty percent of the weight of the facts. As an example, the O. J. Simpson criminal trial ended with a not guilty verdict, but the civil suit that followed found him responsible and heavy monetary damages were assessed.

CHAPTER THREE

Drugs and Alcohol

"To cease smoking is the easiest thing I ever did.
I ought to know, I've done it a thousand times."
                                                    -Mark Twain

Drug testing is becoming a familiar part of life. Employers use them to screen applicants, judges order them as a condition for probation, parents test what they perceive as problem children, and couples going through a divorce demand it from each other in custody battles. The legality and accuracy of the tests depend on whose self-serving interests you listen to: the drug testing companies, the ACLU, or the law profession, just to cite a few.

By driving on a public highway, you implicitly agree to be tested for alcohol if so ordered by the cops, and you may lose your license for one year by refusing to be tested. Many sensitive government and private industry job applicants are required to undergo a drug screen; even rookie cops are tested. Drug and alcohol testing are also mandatory after many types of industrial accidents and, if positive, it may shift the responsibility of the accident to a worker previously thought as a blameless victim.

The accuracy of a drug test depends enormously on the method and the lab performing it. In general, a urine drug screen is just a ballpark evaluation, with a high rate of false positives (meaning the test erroneously shows a drug that is not there), and false negatives (the test fails to detect a drug that is actually present). In most cases the urine is tested nor for a drug itself but for one of the drug's metabolites, or breakdown products of the parent drug. That means that sometimes a drug used two hours before a test may not show up, but marijuana smoked two weeks previously may. Only through blood samples can one measure the precise, on the spot concentration of alcohol or drugs in your body. Urine, breath and other test samples provide just a delayed picture. The most reliable labs use a process called gas chromatography to analyze urine, blood samples, or even hair.

The bottom line: if you do not use drugs but a test is required of you anyway, ask for the most reliable method, the best lab, and request that an additional sample of blood or urine be drawn to be kept sealed and refrigerated for future retesting, to protect you from the occasional false positive result. You may need to provide a list of all the medications you recently ingested since many drugs show "cross-reactivity," and thus, a benign over-the-counter preparation might erroneously be interpreted as an illegal drug.

You may also choose to undergo and pay for additional drug testing at a private lab, ordering that the results be mailed *only* to your attorney. Remember: *client-attorney communications are confidential and can never, ever, be subpoenaed (that is, requested by the courts!)*

A drug user may, instead, prefer the least reliable detection method so that a positive drug screen could later be challenged in court.

There is a booming industry promoting schemes that claim that one may fool a drug screen simply by ingesting a particular compound prior to the test, or by adding certain chemicals to the urine sample. Most of the time this doesn't work, and a sample can easily be checked for adulteration, such as when bleach is added to the urine.

Alcohol

Is it illegal for a minor to purchase alcohol?
Yes! It is a misdemeanor for anyone under 21 to purchase, possess, or consume alcohol. The penalties range from probation to jail time, although first time offenders may be given the alternative of community service. Fines are almost guaranteed and, depending on the state, a minor can have his or her driver's license suspended for up to one year, even if the offense was not traffic related. Just being caught drinking at a party can be enough.

Is it common for a minor to be arrested for drinking?
No, it's not common unless the drinking is related to public intoxication, disorderly conduct, or a traffic violation. A citation and a fine may be issued, but arrests are not the norm.

If arrested, will it go on my record?
The judge may defer making a final decision regarding a conviction for an alcohol offense and may choose to place you on a few months probation instead. If you comply with the judge's request, such as community service or alcohol rehab, the complaint may be dismissed so there is no conviction, but the record for your arrest will persist. A conviction will stay on your criminal record permanently and will likely haunt you forever on job interviews, permit requests, gun licenses, etc.

What if I ask a person older than 21 to buy me alcohol?
Both of you can get in trouble, but the purchaser procuring alcohol for a minor faces potentially harsher penalties and could actually spend time in jail.

What if I use a fake ID to buy alcohol?

In most states it is an infraction to misrepresent your age when purchasing alcohol. To use a fake ID is a misdemeanor, but an overzealous prosecutor may change the accusation from simple deception to forgery if your fake ID looks like a professional job such as one that could easily fool a cop. If you use someone else's name and social security number to obtain a false ID, you could be charged with a felony.

Is it less serious if I use my friend's ID instead?

Not really. If your friend lends you a driver's license to purchase alcohol, both of you may end up with suspended licenses.

Can a minor transport a closed alcohol container?

Only if a parent or a legal guardian is in the vehicle. Adult friends present as passengers in the car don't count. A vehicle used for the illegal transport of alcohol can be seized even if the car does not belong to the driver.

If I'm 21, can I give a beer to my younger brother?

No, but in some states it is legal for someone older than 18 to drink in the presence of a parent or a spouse who's 21 or older.

What is public intoxication? What are the penalties?

Public intoxication charges can be brought against someone who's under the influence of alcohol, illegal substances, or prescription medications, who present a danger to themselves or to others, or are just a plain nuisance. The police officer may choose to issue a citation, instead of taking the individual in, if another adult assumes responsibility for the care and safety of the intoxicated person. If arrested, the person will spend several hours in a holding cell and bond may need to be posted before release, followed then by a court appearance.

Drugs: Illegal stuff

When is it personal use and when is it intent to sell?

That depends on the quantity of drugs you possess, not on the real intent. The law determines specific penalties for possession of each type and amount of controlled substances. Anything considered more than a reasonable amount for personal use can get the person in serious trouble, since it suggests the individual is selling rather than using drugs.

Is it considered "dealing" if my friend pays me for a single marijuana cigarette?

The sale of any illegal substance is considered dealing, and selling a joint at cost, or even one of your own prescription pain pills to a friend who may have a bad toothache, is a crime. If your friend is caught and points the finger in your direction, you could be charged with a felony.

What if I just give the marijuana away instead of selling it?

In most states the charges are usually restricted to simple possession, unless you're older than 18 and your friend is younger than 21, in which case, penalties may be doubled and you may be sentenced to jail for up to one year. Remember also that drug crimes committed within 1,000 feet of school property carry harsher penalties.

Can I be charged if I'm just a passenger in a vehicle where drugs are found?

Yes, you can, depending on the circumstances. Usually the driver of the vehicle is more likely to be charged, but depending on the amount of drugs found in the vehicle and your previous criminal record, you could be arrested and charged.

What if my roommate keeps drugs in our apartment?
Same as above. A clean criminal record and lack of drug history are the most important defenses against possible charges brought against you. However, if the law can prove that you knew of the drug's existence, you could be charged as accessory to the crime.

If I ask, do undercover agents have to tell me they are cops?
That's just an urban myth. Why would they be undercover if they had to tell criminals?

What is entrapment?
When a government official or agency creates a situation that induces a person not otherwise inclined to break the law to actually commit a crime, it is considered entrapment. If, for example, an undercover agent approached you with a large quantity of drugs and you accepted a proposal to distribute it, you could use entrapment as a defense.

Does being intoxicated change the charges for a crime?
An attorney can build an argument for a defendant who was so intoxicated as not to be able to form the intent of a crime. Lesser charges could result in such a case. The defendant may argue ignorance about the possible mental effects of a drug, but this type of defense seldom sways judges and juries.

Is marijuana considered a "real drug"? Can I go to jail?
Despite the controversy over the negative effects of pot, and the fact that alcohol is involved in many more violent crimes and deaths than marijuana, pot it is still considered an illegal drug carrying the same penalties as so-called "hard drugs". Lawmakers and the public in general see pot as a door to the world of illegal drugs, and statistics prove them right (however, the same could be said for cigarette smoking, which is legal).

Since marijuana is the most widely used illegal drug in the country, judges can , at their discretion, be more lenient in setting fines and jail time, especially for first-time offenders. A college student with a clean criminal record found in possession of a small quantity of marijuana may be let go the first time with a "slap on the wrist", but may end up in jail for a second offense.

Can I grow marijuana at home for my own use?
No. It is a felony to cultivate pot even in the privacy of your own home. Depending on the size of your "farm", you could also be charged with cultivating with the intent to sell, which holds much harsher penalties.

Can I legally use pot if I have AIDS or cancer?
Certain states allow licensed medical doctors to prescribe marijuana for medical conditions as long as the prescription is filled by an authorized pharmacy. The whole process is a bureaucratic nightmare, and few patients have access to it. Fortunately for patients who need it, the active chemical ingredient in pot, THC, is available as a prescription pill and readily accessible through most pharmacies, even though it is still labeled as a controlled substance.

Is it a crime to alter the number of pills on my doctor's prescription?
You betcha! It doesn't matter that the doctor mistakenly wrote ten pills instead of the one hundred he said he would, you still can't add a zero to the prescription. If the pharmacist notices any illegal alteration to the prescription, you could be charged with a felony.

What if I request pain pills from two different doctors?
If the prosecutor can prove that you have obtained controlled substances from multiple doctors with the purpose of abuse or diversion (selling or exchanging for other drugs, for example), you could be charged with a felony. In real life, however, it is not uncommon for a patient to inadvertently receive the same or similar medications from two or more doctors, unaware of each other's prescriptions.

Can I go to rehab instead of jail for drug charges?

The judge may let you go to an alcohol and drug rehabilitation facility instead of to jail. This is usually followed by a minimum of several months of probation and community service. The charges could be reinstated if you do not comply with the judge's orders, such as not passing one of the mandatory drug tests or failing to report in as instructed.

Common drugs	Medical Use	Urine Detection (varies with individual)
Amphetamine (Speed)	obesity, sleepiness	2-3 days
Crystal (methamphetamine)	none	2-3 days
Cocaine	local anesthetic	2-3 days
LSD	none	1-4 days
Ecstasy (MDMA)	none	1-3 days
Marijuana	nausea, weight loss	5 days to 2 weeks
Morphine	pain	2-5 days
Heroin	none	2-5 days
Methadone	pain, addiction management	days to weeks
Xanax, Valium	anxiety, panic	days to weeks

CHAPTER FOUR

Sex, Rape, and Harassment

"Sex is important only when you ain't getting any."
-Robin Williams, comedian.

O nce upon a time, in the long forgotten land of black and white movies, Hollywood had a simple rule to deal with sex on the big screen. During filming, a man and a woman lying in bed, each had to have at least one foot touching the floor, which effectively prevented any "hanky-panky". The rules have changed, and the film industry along with advertisers, magazines, and Internet sites have realized that sex sells, (a lot). The American public, and most of the world for that matter, is literally flooded with both open and hidden messages about sex.

Children are becoming sexually active at a much earlier age than their parents, and they are not always emotionally prepared to do so. Unintended teenage pregnancies have reached epidemic proportions, reflecting the explosive combination of hormones and immaturity.

Magazines, TV, and even toys such as the ever-present Barbie dolls, have steadily raised the bar for the perfect body, the ideal kiss, and the uninhibited sexual partner. All this hype sets the stage for the inevitable disappointment when the ultimate relationship does not materialize. For instance, there is now a generation of young boys growing up with video games whose main characters are often voluptuous, seductive women, the likes of which those boys are unlikely to find in adult life.

The line between reality and erotic fantasy is likely to become even more blurred in the future, and who knows, may possibly lead to an increase in the frequency of uninvited advances, and even unintended sexual crimes.

When is it romantic pursuit, and when is it sexual harassment?
If you are a college student who repeatedly sends flowers and cards to a girl who won't even give you the time of day, it is considered romantic pursuit. If you are the girl's teacher and you have the authority to change her grades, the same behavior could be construed as sexual harassment. It has more to do with power than with the pursuit itself, and it does not make a distinction between which gender is pursuing the other. This also applies for same sex harassment.

What is rape?
Rape refers to non-consensual sex (and by sex we mean a myriad of sexual behaviors) when implicit or implied permission was *not* given by one of the partners. It doesn't matter that you and your date have been having sex for years or that you have spent the last hour in foreplay. Any sexual advance beyond the "NO" point could lead to rape charges (rarely, even between husband and wife).

When is consent not valid?
An intoxicated state may preclude someone to give a valid consent. Sex with a female who is too drunk to make a rational decision may be construed as rape. How intoxicated one must be before the partner may be accused of rape is a hotly debated issue. Consent obtained under duress or threat is obviously not valid, and neither is consent given by a minor (see below).

What is statutory rape?
Statutory rape refers to sex between an adult and a minor, defined in most states to be below age either 16 or 18. A minor can't legally give consent, therefore, consensual sex with a minor is not possible. Even if the minor child won't press charges, the parents may in the child's behalf.

If both partners are minors, or they are of similar age, charges are not usually filed. A thirty-year old man and a seventeen-year old girl, however, is a much more difficult case to defend. The fact that she may have lied about her age or she looked older won't change things much.

What if we began to have sex as minors but now I'm 18?
If your partner is older than 16, it is unlikely that you would face charges, but if he or she is younger, you could get in trouble.

Am I liable if I transmit a sexual disease to my partner?
To knowingly inflict a sexually transmitted disease on someone may not only get you sued but could even get you charged with a felony if, for example, AIDS is involved. Your partner would have to prove that you not only *knew* of the diagnosis but also were *aware* of the risks and implications of spreading it to a sexual partner.

Is "streaking" a crime?
Taking your clothes off and running naked across the campus parking lot on a dare, while drunk, may sound like an innocuous prank, but it may get you arrested for indecent exposure. If convicted you should be able to get off just by paying a fine and possibly doing some community service.

The nightmare comes if you end up included in the public database that lists sex offenders by names and current addresses. This database was designed to protect communities from sexual predators, and it is accessible to your family, neighbors, and your boss. Indecent exposure is considered a sex offense and after a seemingly innocent "streaking" episode, your name may be listed on that database, side by side with the name of a seedy guy who walks around naked under a raincoat, exposing himself to little children.

CHAPTER FIVE

Credit, Bad Credit, and Bankruptcy

"If you can count your money,
you don't have a billion dollars."
-J. Paul Getty, Billionaire

Even before graduating from high school, a student may be inundated with offers for easy access to money, mainly from credit card companies. Their marketing experts have found that if they can get you "hooked" on a certain brand of card early on, you are likely to continue with the same brand in the future. This ploy has also been used for years by the tobacco and automobile companies who have established a marketing truth: consumers are very loyal to a specific brand, and they tend to remain a "Marlboro man" or a "Ford aficionado" forever.

The bank and other financial institutions take a calculated risk when they mail credit cards to complete strangers. This is because they know beforehand that young adults are more impulsive, not able to restrain their purchases, and may incur more debt than they can afford. It doesn't really matter to the credit companies that some people will never be able to pay their balance on the card because it's all included in the cost of doing business, and in the hope of earning interest on any unpaid balances.

It does, however, matter to a person who is a student on a low paying job and who may start his or her adult life with bad credit. Generally, being labeled as a credit risk will cost a person money through higher interest rates, extra percentage "points" to obtain a loan, and even credit refusal. The world is full of ads for "no money down", "bad credit accepted", and "easy lay-away". Be careful. Cash is still king.

Anybody may develop financial difficulties, even the rich. It could arise from the loss of one's job, health problems, compulsive shopping or gambling, drug use, and many other reasons. There are, however, appropriate ways to deal with debt in a responsible manner.

Do I need a credit card?

Not really. Even though a credit card is convenient and can provide a quick loan, unless you can pay it in full by the end of the month, the interest rates are usually exorbitant (even if they seem reasonable for the first few months). Be sure and read the fine print.

A sensible alternative is to get a debit card. You open a bank account, say with $500.00, and the debit card allows you to spend only that amount of money. No bounced checks, no debt, no interest, and, depending on the bank, you may even earn some interest in the account balance.

How do I establish a good credit history?

Real simple: pay on time. The repayments of a car loan, a home mortgage, or even a student loan reflect whether you are credit worthy. Having a credit card and paying the balance properly also count. Repeat delays or defaults on a loan are a no-no. Opening one or more bank or savings accounts may serve as a future source of reference for credit (usually three good sources of credit are requested).

If I get divorced, will my husband's previous credit history apply to me?

Probably only the bad stuff. If a couple has been labeled as a "bad credit risk", divorce or separation seldom improves either one's credit. On the other hand, if the ex-husband has a good credit history, a recently divorced wife may not be included in it. She may need to rebuild her credit since the wife often has less visible participation in financial decisions. A couple may choose to carry separate bank and credit card accounts so each can build an independent credit profile.

What do credit bureau companies do?

These are private organizations that collect data on you and your credit history and, for a fee, they sell this data to other companies. For example, if you apply for a credit card at a department store, they will check with one of these credit bureaus before issuing you a card. If you are seen as a poor credit risk, your request will be denied, which may influence future credit applications, as this information goes into your permanent file.

A credit report usually contains your name, social security number, address, and employment history, as well as your spouse's name and home ownership. Debts, foreclosures, and any previous credit inquiry will be posted there, too. Most people are surprised to see what is in their credit history. The expression "Big Brother" comes to mind.

Poor credit ratings may stay in your record file for seven years, but bankruptcy won't be erased for ten years. If you have been denied credit because of a report from a credit bureau, you have the right to obtain the information contained on your file for free, within sixty days. You can always obtain your file by paying a small fee to the credit bureau. If you find an error in the report, you can write them (within a reasonable period of time) and demand that it be corrected or altogether erased from your records.

What if I can't pay my debts?
This is more common than you think. People frequently get overextended, many times because of unforeseen circumstances. There are agencies, some not-for-profit such as the Consumer Credit Counseling Service (www.nfcc.org), that will help you consolidate and prioritize your debts.

Prioritizing means paying the important stuff first, food and mortgage being the obvious ones, and paying the car loan if you need it to work. Remember that when it rains it pours, so try to keep your health insurance also.

Note that nowadays you can't go to jail for failure to pay your debts. Your debtors may easily repossess any secured loans (like a car or furniture), but it is more difficult for them to collect unsecured loans (like a credit card debt).

What happens in bankruptcy?

When filing for bankruptcy you essentially admit that your debt can't be resolved in any other way, and you ask for legal protection in order to start again. The courts will then erase most, if not all, of your unsecured debts although a creditor will still be able to repossess any secured loan, such as a car. This is one reason to pay your secured loans prior to the unsecured ones, such as a credit card debt.

Filing for bankruptcy will haunt you for at least ten years, and it will make it next to impossible to obtain an unsecured loan or a credit card for that period of time. There are different "chapters" in bankruptcy, each one designed to solve a particular situation, such as dealing with individuals, corporations etc.

Can credit collectors harass me?

Credit collectors primarily deal with guilt since they know that most people are honest and don't want a "bad credit report". Phone calls and threatening letters are the main methods they use, but it is illegal to harass you. Some forms of harassment include:

- Contacting your friends, boss, or relatives
- Calling you at work, if it jeopardizes your job
- Calling repeatedly or late at night
- Threatening calls or profane language
- Making false or misleading statements
- Publishing your name on a debtor's list

You can easily stop the credit collectors simply by writing them using certified mail with return receipt, stating that you refuse to pay the debt, or you disagree that you owe it, and request they stop contacting you. By law they have to do so, and their next recourse will be to sue you in court. You may sue a collection agency if they break the law regarding harassment.

What if I can't pay my doctor's bills?

Well, doctors have the right to refuse to treat non-paying patients. Most of them, however, are sympathetic to poor sick folks and they will continue to treat them provided they don't feel they are being taken advantage of.

Bring some proof that you are in a financial bind. Ask for a discount (this is often accepted), offer to pay a reasonable monthly sum, or even barter some of your skills for the doctor's (do his lawn work in exchange for the gall bladder removal you need). Don't forget to ask for medication samples since drugs are often the most expensive part of a medical visit.

CHAPTER SIX

Renting a House

Happiness is having a large, loving, caring, close-knit family... in another city.
George Burns, comedian

You're young, you always lived with your parents or in a college dorm, and now you feel it is time to move out, to have your own space, your own apartment. So you and three of your buddies come up with enough cash for the first three month's rental and a commitment from each other to stay together for at least one year. Simple, eh? Of course you are forgetting that one of you will be the "main person" to sign the lease, and that utilities cost much more than you imagined. Cable TV and high speed Internet connection come at a price, and somebody flooded the apartment by leaving the tub faucet open and now there's no extra cash to fix it. One of your buddies regularly fails to pay his share of the rent and the other routinely opens your mail, while the third empties his wastebasket through the window. The "nice" landlord decides that he wants more money for the additional nuisance and since you never really read the contract to begin with, you may have to fork over the extra cash. Farfetched you say? Not really.

Renting an apartment is the first real world responsibility most people experience besides holding a summer job. It involves planning, accountability, and good judgment. It means not only *reading* the lease contract, but also *understanding* it. Boring, boring, boring, but it may prevent a lot of future headaches.

Buying a home brings with it a whole new set of problems and responsibilities, and it is better left for those who have already experienced renting.

Do I need to pay to fill out a rental application?

Most landlords will charge you $20-$50 to cover the cost of checking you out. This may include fees for a credit service bureau and rental databases where deadbeats are listed. This money may be refundable if you rent the apartment.

How do they screen applicants?

Applicants are primarily screened on their ability to pay. A bad credit report may keep you from getting the apartment, and so can a criminal record. Landlords may chose not to rent to college students or pet owners, but they can't refuse to lease based on race, gender, religion, or ethnic origin.

Why do they need a security deposit? Do I get it back?

A security deposit is a guarantee that enough money will be left at the end of the lease to repair any damage beyond normal "wear-and-tear". Any amount not used for repairs is refunded to the tenant at the end of the contract.

It's a good idea to take some pictures of the interior of the premises before you move in. It will document the original state of the building in case of a disagreement about damages.

What is usually contained on a lease agreement?

- A term, or lease period
- Name or names of residents
- Restrictions regarding subleasing the property
- Inclusion or exclusion of utilities
- Alterations to the premises
- Landlord's right to inspect the premises
- General expected behavior
- Penalties for violations, such as charging a fee for late payment
- Renewal

Is an oral agreement enough?

This is asking for trouble. Misunderstandings are common even if the landlord is a member of the family.

Can the landlord inspect the premises after I move in?

Definitely. It has to be done at reasonable hours and preferably after the landlord announces his or her plans to inspect the premises. In case of a real or perceived emergency, the landlord may enter the building at any time. There is a fine line between the tenant's right to privacy and the landlord's right to inspect his or her building. If, during the inspection, the landlord finds improper use of the premises or signs of criminal activity, he may take action immediately.

What are my rights as a tenant?

- A livable space, clean, and relatively free of noise
- Privacy
- Repairs done in a timely fashion

What are my obligations?

- Pay the rent on time
- Behave responsibly
- Care for the premises
- Communicate any problems to the landlord

Can I withhold the rent if the landlord fails to fix the apartment?

No, this constitutes grounds for eviction. If the landlord does not perform a repair in a timely fashion after two requests have been mailed, and the repairs are important for your health, not just cosmetic, you may hire a professional to perform the work and deduct it from the rent. Keep all receipts and never withhold the regular rent. All communications should be sent by registered mail, return receipt. Always keep a copy of the letters you send to the landlord in case you must defend your actions at a later date.

Can I sublease the apartment?

Read your lease, if not forbidden you may sublease it. Don't forget to get the other tenants sharing the apartment to sign a contract. This is for your own protection.

Should all roommates pay the same share?

A more equitable way is to auction off the most desirable room(s). If there are four people and four rooms, one of the tenants may be willing to pay more than one-fourth of the total rental price for the privilege of a room with, lets say, a private bathroom. If this is done with all the rooms, the tenant who gets the least desirable room may end up paying substantially less than one fourth of the rent.

What if I can't pay the rent anymore?

You are still responsible for the duration of the contract. If you have a month-to-month agreement, no problem, but if you still have another eighteen months to go, one alternative is to negotiate with the landlord a lump sum for ending the lease early. You can also sublet the apartment or assign the whole lease to a new tenant, if allowed by the contract.

The landlord may choose to sue you for non-payment and if you still don't pay, your earnings could be garnished and your assets used to pay the debt for up to ten years afterwards. You may even be "blacklisted", or included in a renter's list of deadbeat tenants, reducing your chances of renting another apartment or house in the future.

CHAPTER SEVEN

College

"Fat, drunk, and stupid
is no way to go through life, son."
- Dean Wormer, from the movie Animal House

Finally, college! After all the awkward years in high school, finally, a chance to reinvent oneself. No more labels. I can start from scratch, I can be myself. Freedom, parties, co-ed dorms, and no parents in sight with built-in radars. I can do whatever I want.

Yes, you can, as long as you don't get caught. You have to contend now, not only with the American judicial system, but also the sometimes arcane rules and regulations of a college. To make it even worse, political correctness permeates the academic environment and adds another layer of policies. If you expect a worry-free environment, you won't find it in most colleges. There are rules governing even the appearance of impropriety. Some colleges go as far as posting rules about what is considered appropriate behavior for dating.

Sex, drugs, and alcohol, often associated with a college student's period of experimentation, are heavily regulated. Specific codes of conduct exist in most schools and disregard for these codes may result in penalties ranging from simple reprimands to college expulsion (and criminal prosecution when warranted).

Is hazing illegal?

Hazing in its many forms is illegal. Any intentional physical or mental harm induced under the label of hazing is a crime. You could be charged with a misdemeanor or even a felony if serious injury or death results from an act of hazing.

Hazing is a crime even if the person being hazed consents to it. Furthermore, anyone who has first-hand knowledge of hazing, and does not report it to school authorities could also be charged, as well as any organization, (such as a fraternity or sorority), that promotes or tolerates it.

Can my dorm be searched by college officials?

Yes, no need for prior notice. A college has to comply with fire safety rules that include inspection. By accepting to live on campus you give up the right to privacy as far as searches are concerned. If unauthorized or illegal items are found, the college officials have the option of removing the objects without your authorization, and additional fines, probation, or even expulsion may occur. Firearms or hard drugs in a dorm will likely get you expelled, and criminal charges may be added.

What if they find a six-pack in a minor's dorm?

In most campuses this is considered a serious offense, even if the containers are empty. In fact an empty alcohol container used as "decoration" in a dorm could be considered an infraction.

Fines and probation are likely, but seldom are more serious charges filed. Repeat offenders or individuals perceived by officials as troublemakers may, however, receive harsher penalties at the discretion of the school.

CHAPTER EIGHT

Wills, Trusts, and Power of Attorney

"I'm gonna live forever"
-From the title song of the movie "Fame"

You don't need a will; only your family or heirs do. If you are planning to live forever, a will is not necessary, but if you die without a will (intestate, they call it), the government decides what happens to your estate (your "stuff"), and even to your small children if both parents die. Your kids may end up with "Uncle Joe" who drinks too much, has bad breath, and likes little girls, or some other weird or sick relative. A will allows you to reach beyond the grave to choose the best options for your loved ones.

The law has a number of other instruments such as trusts and power-of-attorney, designed to facilitate the execution of one's wishes in a world bound by legal constraints.

Most of the following chapter may seem useless to young people, just starting their lives. It does however help understand what their parents and relatives may have established in case of death or disability that will possibly influence the young person's life.

What do I need to draw a will?

Not much. Most states require that the will be typed (computer forms are fine). In several states you can do it by hand, as long as the whole will is handwritten by you and signed, called a holographic will.

You have to be 18 or older and of sound mind. One or more beneficiaries should be named as well as an executor. You should sign and date it in front of two people, not named in the will, as witnesses.

You can make a will as complicated as you wish but a simple sentence like, "I leave all my assets to my spouse," constitutes a valid will, as long as the items above are followed.

What does the executor do?

The executor, who often is also one of the beneficiaries in a will, makes sure that the wishes expressed in the will are properly carried out. The executor has the power to decide any items left unclear by the will, but in most cases, the executor has to hire an attorney to go through probate.

What is probate?

This refers to the legal proceedings by the courts necessary to validate and implement a will after the person dies. It can be a bureaucratic nightmare: slow, inefficient and costly, often consuming a significant portion of the estate for attorney's fees and delaying its distribution to the rightful heirs by months or even years. The assets of the deceased may be frozen after his or her death until probate is concluded, and serious financial problems are not uncommon for an already grieving family.

How can I avoid probate?

Any bank or brokerage account can be opened with a "right of survivorship" clause, meaning that you can designate the person(s) entitled to that account, portfolio, or part of your estate as soon as a death certificate is produced. The paperwork is simple and it is usually done at the bank or brokerage firm itself when you open an account. Life insurance is another good way to bypass probate, since the beneficiary of that insurance is entitled to receive the money without any legal delays.

What is a trust? Can I use it instead of a will?

The idea is simple: you put all your toys (or assets) in a "box" called a trust. You can play with the toys, sell or exchange them whenever you want, and after you die, the toy box with all its belongings becomes the property of your designated heirs.

A trust is basically a private document (as opposed to a will which is public) that allows you to transfer ownership of your assets to a legal entity while retaining the rights over them. Once you place your assets in a trust, technically you don't own them anymore, therefore they are not subject to probate after you die. A revocable trust (as opposed to an irrevocable trust) can be modified or cancelled anytime if you change your mind, go through a divorce, or any other life changes. A trust is, many times, the preferred way to avoid paying taxes on the inheritance, the so called "death taxes."

The disadvantage of a trust is that it may be costly to prepare and it does require yearly tax returns, incurring further expenses from accountants and attorneys.

Do I need a living will?

Do you want to be kept alive by machines if a coma is irreversible? Unless you have a living will, your relatives, doctors, hospitals, and attorneys may make that decision. In a living will, you formalize your wishes regarding health, long term care, organ donation, and life support in case you are unable to make a decision yourself. Standard forms for a living will can be obtained at any hospital.

What is a power of attorney?

It is a legal document that authorizes another person to act on your behalf. You may use it to authorize someone to sell a house, rent property, cash checks, and almost anything you could otherwise do yourself. You may prefer to limit the scope of the power of attorney to a single task and for a predetermined period of time, or else the agent could conceivably act without your consent, or even against your best interest. A good friend or even a family relative who develops a financial misfortune or a drug problem could cause some serious damage with the use of a broad, unlimited power of attorney.

A *durable* power of attorney is permanent until revoked, even if the individual becomes incapacitated or unable to make his or her own decisions. A *springing* power of attorney may, on the other hand, be drafted to become active only if incapacitation of the person occurs.

CHAPTER NINE

Small Claims, Mediation, and Arbitration

"I was never ruined but twice - once when I lost a lawsuit, and once when I gained one."
- Voltaire

The American courts are relatively inefficient and sluggish in large part due to the sheer volume of cases. The number of pending criminal cases are staggering, jails are overcrowded, and many who belong behind bars are still roaming the streets. Civil cases also choke the courts with tens of thousands of pending cases, in part due to a society that's litigation-happy and fueled by some huge, high profile monetary settlements. Alternatives to a regular lawsuit exist that provide a prompt, less costly option to the judge-jury-lawyer system.

Small claims court, and alternative dispute resolution (ADR for short), which includes mediation and arbitration, are relatively pain free ways to resolve a civil dispute, and they should be considered whenever litigation is an option.

Small claims court involves a judge but not a jury, and in many cases, no attorney is involved. Both parties may agree to represent themselves without many of the formalities of a regular court.

Mediation occurs when two opposing parties choose an impartial individual to aid in helping them settle a dispute on their own.

Arbitration works more like a regular court, but a private one. Instead of waiting for a court date, both parties choose one or more arbitrators, often from a list of retired judges, and they agree to abide by the decision of the arbitrator. This is a more formal process than mediation, and both parties present their cases in a more "legalistic" way than during mediation. The decision reached by the parties involved usually carries legal weight by previous agreement.

What kind of cases do small claims courts handle?

Usually small claims deal with monetary disputes, such as, a roommate who refuses to pay his or her portion of the rent, or restitution of an object, for example, the return of an engagement ring if the wedding was called off.

Some states like Tennessee don't have small claims court. A General Sessions Court handles many of the same type of cases but it is more formal and follows many of the judicial procedure rules.

Is there a monetary "cap" in small claims court?

Each state has a maximum amount that can be recovered. The average cap is $5,000.

How do I file a claim?

In general a claim has to be filed in small claims court, within a year of discovery, in the court closest to the party you are suing. A case may also be filed near the place the incident occurred, such as a fender-bender. Out-of-state cases may become a financial drain and not worth the money one could recoup.

What happens in court?

Both parties will present their case bringing with them any pertinent evidence such as receipts, pictures, witnesses, or affidavits. The judge will usually ask questions to both parties, and a decision then reached shortly afterwards.

Whether you are a plaintiff or a defendant, try to present your case in a professional, succinct, and respectful manner. Avoid being too emotional. Remember that the judge hears cases all day long and usually is in no mood for lengthy descriptions, unimportant details, or displays of anger.

What if I am sued in small claims court?

You will receive a summons with the court date. Unless you show up, you will lose by default and a judgment will be placed against you.

The cases are usually heard within weeks of being filed, and you may not have much time to prepare your defense.

If I win, how do I collect?

With a favorable judgment in hand, you can get your money from the other person's assets or wages, but you have to do it yourself. The courts won't do it for you. If the other party has no income or assets at present, you may choose to wait to collect the award since a judgment may be enforceable for ten years or more.

When should I try mediation?

Mediation works well if you are trying to remain in good terms with the other party, such as your neighbor or an ex-girlfriend. A good mediator is a facilitator, a good listener, a priest, and a psychologist, allowing the parties to vent their frustrations and anger, while providing a solid base upon which an agreement can be built. The ideal mediation allows each party to leave the table feeling like they both won, or both lost.

How do I choose a mediator?

Most large cities have mediation centers that can be readily found in the phone book or on the Internet. Both parties have to accept the mediator as someone they see as impartial, since the main goal of mediation is to reach a mutual agreement.

Is mediation binding?

No. Mediation does not end with a judgment and carries no legal weight. However, if an agreement has been reached in good faith, the courts may treat it as a contract.

When is arbitration a choice?

Suppose you bought a car that turned out to be a "lemon". After exhausting the regular complaint avenues, you may choose to sue the dealer in court, which may take months or years, and will probably cost in attorney fees alone, more than the price of the vehicle itself. Or, you can choose arbitration as a process that is speedier, and much, much less expensive.

Both parties may choose an arbitrator from a list, and then the two chosen ones may select a third member to form a panel. Prior to arbitration, both parties must agree in writing that the decision is binding, with pre-established penalties in case the contract is broken.

CHAPTER TEN

Jobs

"A lot of fellows nowadays have a B.A., M.D., or Ph.D.
Unfortunately, they don't have a J.O.B."
- Fats Domino

Every time you turn on the TV, you see young, beautiful people with sharp clothes and fancy cars. They live the good life, they have nice homes, they party ALL the time, and you never see them work! Count me in. I also "want my MTV, money for nothing and the chicks for free." But, alas, an honest person has to work to be able to enjoy the good life. Frankly, it's a lousy deal, because by the time you finish your day's work you may be too tired to party, and besides, you have to wake up early the next morning…to work!

Youth poses an additional obstacle when looking for work, since most desirable job skills are acquired through time and experience, unavailable to a young person. Showing up for work on-time every day, part of the so-called "work ethics", may not be easy for someone who never goes to bed before 4 A.M.. The discipline to hold a job is just one of the basic requirements for a good paying gig. Remember, there is nothing in the constitution that says "…the pursuit of happiness and an easy, high paying job."

The solution is to start from the bottom, learning the necessary skills for better pay and more satisfying positions. Making $7.50/hr sounds great if you are young and single, but as you "mature" and the kids all of a sudden need braces, it's a dismal salary. The longer you stay in school (learning), the better the chances that you will be able to pick-and-choose your career and your own path.

Along the way, you will find that there is a legal tug-of-war between the rights of the employers and the employees, leading to suits on discrimination, sexual harassment, on-the-job injuries, and many others. This means that from the moment you apply for a job, you and your prospective employer may perceive each other as legal targets. Not the best start for a long, fruitful career.

In this work environment it is as important to know your rights as it is to know when not to exercise them. A certain dose of flexibility, compassion, and understanding of each other's unique problems is mandatory whether you are a married couple or trying to maintain a healthy employer-employee relationship. Nothing will poison a marriage or a job faster than turning to legal recourses rather than open dialogue and good sense.

What can they ask me during a job interview?

In general, they can ask you anything related to your capacity to perform the job, including previous experience, references, and criminal records. The employer may require job-skill tests to verify whether you are qualified to perform a specific task, such as determining how many words-per-minute you can type or whether you can operate an eighteen-wheeler.

They may *not* ask you about your age, sex, sexual orientation, religion, color, ethnicity, or anything that could lead to discrimination. They may not ask you which associations or clubs you belong to. However, a good interviewer can easily find loopholes by asking the prospective employee "tricky questions" such as the date you graduated from high school, which is a dead giveaway of your age.

Can my previous boss blacklist me?

Your old boss can't give your prospective employer references that contain unsubstantiated information, nor can he give away personal information about you, such as mentioned above. This includes race, ethnicity, etc.

References that contain false accusations such as fraud can lead to a lawsuit for defamation, but in real life, an ex-boss can utilize more subtle ways to smear someone's reputation. A simple, "I'd rather not discuss it", used to answer a question about the honesty of a prospective employee can be damaging enough.

Can they discriminate based on my appearance?

Yes, they may. A pierced tongue, a large tattoo on the neck, or purple hair can be a legitimate reason to be denied a job that deals with the public. In general, a self-inflicted change in appearance is not treated the same as a cosmetic defect, such as a large facial mole or baldness.

Can they make me take a physical examination and a drug screen?

Yes, but in most states you will be required to submit to a physical exam (which usually requires a drug screen) only after you have been offered a job. The offer may be withdrawn if you don't pass the physical. If a disability is detected during the physical examination, which would not impair your ability to perform the occupation you have been offered, you can't legally be denied that job.

What is the probation period?

This is the *dating* period, lasting from a few weeks to a few months, between employer and employee to find out if they are both happy with the choices made. During that time, either party may terminate their association without the need for a specific reason. A worker on probation may not be eligible to the same rights as the permanent employees.

If hired, do I get to sign a contract?

It depends on the company's policy. Some employers will hire you as an "at-will-employee", meaning there is no formal contract. Therefore, you may quit or be fired at any time, provided no discrimination is involved.

Some employers use contracts and manuals that specify conditions for work, dismissal, discipline, and many other items ranging from dress code to absenteeism. Most often a contract protects the employer more than the employee. No matter how restrictive a contract is, one can't waive his or her rights as a worker, such as the right to adequate compensation, consideration for promotions, and accommodations for disabilities.

Can a contract keep me from accepting a similar job at another place?

Yes. A contract may stipulate that after you leave your present place of employment, you can't divulge any "trade secrets" such as financial information or production methods, or you may face heavy fines. Furthermore, a contract may include a "non-compete" clause that bars you from accepting a similar job at another company for a period of time, usually one year, within a predetermined geographical area. Such a clause can't be made so restrictive that a person can't make a living at all, otherwise the courts will rule it invalid. For instance, a dentist may sign a contract to work for a large dental office provided that, for a period of one year, when he or she leaves that office, the dentist agrees not to establish an independent practice within twenty-five miles of the previous location. A contract that stipulated, let's say, a restrictive radius of one hundred miles for the duration of five years would probably not be enforceable.

What happens if I get injured on the job?

Most large employers carry worker's compensation insurance, which covers injuries and illnesses that occur on the job. This insurance is designed to cover both the necessary medical care, as well as lost wages that may ensue as a consequence, due to inability to perform one's job. You have to inform the company, in writing, about the injury and the circumstances as soon as you can. Worker's compensation may not cover accidents related to a person's own fault, such as willful disregard for safety rules or impaired judgment due to alcohol or drug use. A drug and alcohol screen is often mandatory when a job related accident occurs.

During the time you are unable to work, you may receive compensation, in general two-thirds of your salary (tax-free). This benefit ceases when the treating physician feels the worker has reached maximum improvement.

The worker's compensation system is frequently an adversarial situation, a battle involving the worker, the insurance company, the employer, and often a lawyer. Some workers choose to "milk the system" for all they can, exaggerating their complaints for monetary gains. It is not unusual for such a worker to be kept under secret videotape surveillance by the insurance company. On the other hand, some doctors, pressured by the employer, may allow patients to return to work before they are fully recovered.

What if I don't recover enough to return to my previous job?

If the worker can't return to a previously held occupation, he or she may be reassigned by the employer to another job that fits the worker's disabilities *if* such a job is available. In that case, the worker is entitled to receive the difference in salary if the new job is of a lesser pay than the previous one. The employer, however, has no duty to create a *new* position to accommodate the injured person, and the worker may be legally fired if no position is available.

Do I receive compensation if I sustain a permanent injury?

Yes. The loss of a limb or an eye, or any proven diminished capacity for work may entitle the worker to monetary compensation. There are special medical books filled with tables that assign a number to each part of the injured person's anatomy as a percentage of the whole body, and this number is used to calculate the injured worker's award.

What happens if I get injured on my way to work?

If you have an accident while driving as part of your job, the injuries resulting from it are covered under worker's compensation. If you are just going to or from work, tough luck! Your regular medical insurance should still provide the necessary health coverage.

What if my work environment is making me sick?

In general, you can't be compensated if the lights, smells or vapors in the surroundings make you sick unless you can prove that a listed toxic item is present in the environment, and that other employees have also become ill.

Is there a financial "safety net" if I get fired?

If you lose your job, you may be eligible for unemployment benefits for a period not to exceed twenty-six weeks. Exceptions that may make a person ineligible include workers who are too sick to work and those who refuse a reasonable job offer. The same is true for those who are fired for misconduct, as well as, for workers who just quit their job.

Benefits vary from state to state but rarely do they exceed half of the person's regular wages. Each state has a cap on a minimum and a maximum amount of benefits that a worker may receive, ranging from $200 to $400/week. It is a crime to hold a job while receiving unemployment benefits, and, if caught, the worker may have to pay restitution and fines and may even spend time in jail.

CHAPTER ELEVEN

Traveling Abroad

*"I met a lot of people in Europe.
I even encountered myself."*
- James Baldwin, Writer

Traveling to another country can be a great way to expand your mind. Different cultures, remarkable sights, unusual smells and tastes, all combine to spice up and enrich your life like few other experiences can.

It may also become one of your biggest nightmares, if you land in a foreign jail. For example, many young adults choose "spring break" as their first occasion to travel overseas. Mexico has surpassed many Florida cities as the target for sun, girls, boys, and beer. The search for excitement can override good sense, and the freedom experienced when one is away from home compounds to the problem. People, young and old, often forget that several of the laws previously mentioned in this book do not apply to many countries, and very few nations respect a person's legal rights in the same way the U.S. does.

Ignorance or disregard for local laws and customs land a few thousand Americans in foreign jails every year, many on drug charges. In some countries, possession of even a small amount of illegal drugs may be punishable by death. You may be held in a foreign jail for months before a trial is set, hard labor is the norm, and solitary confinement is a common occurrence.

Remember: American laws do not apply overseas!

Leaving the Country

What do I need before traveling abroad?

A common advice: take twice the money and half the clothes. We also highly recommend getting a passport, even if a birth certificate may be acceptable to enter some countries. You may obtain a passport at any post office for a small fee, but it will cost you more if you are in a hurry. Make copies of your passport: carry one with you and give one to a companion. If you lose your passport, a simple duplicate may expedite a new one at the local American consulate. Before departing verify if the country you're traveling to requires an entry visa.

Inform friends of your itinerary before departing and contact them periodically. Remember that e-mail is not available everywhere and phone calls can be exorbitantly expensive, especially if done from the hotel room. "Call-back" cards often offer a much cheaper alternative to hotel phone charges.

Leave at home any credit cards you won't be using during the trip. If traveling with your spouse, make sure each one carries a different brand or digit of credit card in case one of you is robbed; if you call to report a stolen credit card, all the other cards sharing the same number will be cancelled. Use traveler's checks when possible, and keep the serial numbers in a safe place. Money belts work really well in holding large denomination bills.

Keep medications in their original bottles. If using prescription narcotics, it may be a good idea to carry a letter from your doctor.

What precautions should I take after I arrive?

Leave most valuables including the passport in the hotel safe. A "do not disturb" sign on the door will likely discourage thieves, while a "clean room, please" sign will do the opposite.

Be continuously aware of your surroundings, and trust your instincts. Pickpockets are everywhere, usually working in pairs. One is there to create a distraction while the other steals your valuables. Backpacks (or large billfolds), and crowded places such as subways, make an irresistible combination for thieves. American tourists are also fairly easy to spot both by their demeanor, as well as, the way they dress (chewing gum and tennis shoes are good clues).

In some countries, dishonest cab drivers have been known to take unsuspecting passengers to a remote location and rob them. When possible, use taxis from a reputable local company. It is usually safer to get a cab at the hotel than on the street.

Do not accept packages from strangers, even if it is "just a little something for my sister in New York". Watch your luggage and pack it yourself. If somebody slips something into your bag, you're guilty until proven otherwise.

Memorize the name and location of your hotel and carry a card with the information in your wallet. It is not difficult to forget the name and address of one's hotel during a long multi-city trip. Imagine going out for a stroll in a foreign city, after leaving your luggage at the hotel and not having a clue about where to return!

What will get me in trouble?

A) Excessive drinking. Cheap liquor and a barman that doesn't know what an I.D. is can rapidly escalate from a good time, to a bar fight with the locals.

B) Drugs. "Hey gringo, wanna buy some pot"? Cons or corrupted cops may use drug offers as a form of entrapment. One-third of all Americans arrested abroad are in jail on drug charges.

C) Sex. Statutory rape is as illegal there as it is here.

What do I do if I get arrested?

Call the American consulate first. They may help by providing you with a list of English-speaking attorneys, and they may call your family in the States. They can't give you money and they certainly can't get you out of jail.

Although we can't condone it, bribery is rampant in the judicial system and jails of many underdeveloped countries. Money may buy you a safer cell away from violent criminals, better food, and sometimes even freedom. When confronted with bogus charges from corrupt officers trying to extort money, do your best not to go to jail. You can always file a formal complaint later, when you're safely back on U.S. soil.

What can I bring back to the U.S.?

You can bring up to $400 in foreign goods without paying taxes. Do not bring drugs, illegally bought antiques or any vegetables or fruits. The first will get you in jail; the others may lead to heavy fines.

What are my rights regarding the airlines?

There are several ways an airline can spoil your vacation. One is to "bump" you by overselling seats. If denied boarding, you are entitled to compensation which increases in value depending on the length of time you have to wait for the next flight. You may request vouchers for food, phone calls, hotel, and transportation if stranded overnight.

If your flight arrives late for reasons other than inclement weather, and that delay causes you to miss the next leg of your flight, the airline has to find you a seat on the same or another airline, on a non-stop flight to your destination, at the earliest available time. This is generally known as *Rule 240*, and each airline has its own variation on the rules.

A cell phone is a great aid if a flight has been cancelled. You should use it while still in line at the counter, waiting to be rebooked on another flight. Reserve the flight yourself using the airline's toll-free number (don't forget to obtain a confirmation number), thus getting ahead of the many, many fellow passengers in front of you. When you reach the counter simply tell them about your new reservation and ask for a voucher to pay for it, if using a different airline. If they give you a hard time, ask to speak to a supervisor. Do not raise your voice, and try to remain composed. Tired and stressed airline agents may convince the airport security to remove a demanding passenger from the ticket counter, just by labeling the person as unruly.

CHAPTER TWELVE

Citizenship

"Do the right thing.
It will gratify some people and astonish the rest."
—Mark Twain

The United States in its present form is based on a 200 year-plus constitution that has survived against formidable odds. The result has been a unique democratic society that has grown and prospered, effectively raising the bar for other democratic nations. It has been said, however, that eternal vigilance is the price of freedom, and the constitution empowers all of us with rights and obligations that allow us to preserve our way of life.

The ultimate price American citizens have paid for freedom is the reason we remain a Union and why our official language is not German. Smaller requests to keep this democracy alive are made everyday to most of us. Many times just a nuisance, sometimes a major sacrifice, a citizen's rights and obligations frequently overlap, raising questions about moral and ethical decisions.

Voting and jury duty generally pose no major ethical dilemma. Military service can be a contentious point. Gun ownership though, is a major divisive issue in this country and we are not naïve enough to endorse, in this book, neither the NRA nor the Brady people. We may discuss what our forefathers meant by the "right to bear arms" until we turn blue and never reach a conclusion. The truth is that while hunting accidents are a relatively small problem, death and injuries by firearms are a true epidemic in this nation. Even countries such as Israel, where much of the population carry sub-machine guns, have one-tenth the death rate by firearms compared to the United States. Go figure.

Armed Forces

What is Selective Service registration?
President Carter reintroduced selective service registration in 1980. It allows for military readiness by informing the government the number of available men in case of war. Registering does not mean that you are enlisting. Even if a war erupts, a lottery based on one's birthday and other factors will determine who will be drafted.

Who must register?
All males must register within 30 days of their 18th birthday. If you have not registered one month after your birthday, you are breaking the law. Females are exempt.

You may receive a card around your birthday reminding you to register. You may do it at the Post Office, by mail, or even at the many high schools that provide that service. If you have access to the Internet, you may do it on-line.

What if I don't register?
Registration is a requirement for Federal student aid and most Federal jobs. In extreme cases you could be prosecuted and slapped with penalties of up to $250,000 fine and five years in jail. You can't register at all if you have not done it by age 26. Many doors may close if you do not register.

What if I choose to enlist in the armed forces?
You have to be 18 (or 17, with your parents permission), you must have finished high school or have an equivalency diploma, and you must pass a basic aptitude test, as well as, a physical examination.

What are my rights as an enlisted member?

Once you enlist, your rights are sharply curtailed, and you essentially "belong" to the military for an assigned period of time. You are subject to martial law instead of the normal judicial system, a structure with a whole new set of regulations.

Military service can provide the right person with an honorable career, expert training, camaraderie and many other benefits (an enlisted person, for example, may legally purchase alcohol before becoming 21). Military service is not, however, for everybody (see below).

What if I enlisted and now I have changed my mind?

Your best chances to leave the military are within the first 180 days of enrollment, considered to be entry-level status. You must quickly bring to the attention of your commanding officer the reasons for leaving the military so the discharge process may be initiated. For instance, if you enlisted at 17 and did not have your parent's consent, you may qualify for discharge.

There are several other reasons for military separation, including:

a) Homosexuality. "Don't ask, don't tell." You may not admit having had homosexual relations, but you may ask to be discharged because you wish to have homosexual contact.

b) Physical disability. You may find, after enlisting, that you suffer from a physical disability that keeps you from performing your military obligations.

c) Hardship. If you become responsible for your family's financial or health care.

d) Conscientious objection. After enlisting you realize that, you will be unable to harm or kill another person in battle.

e) Personality disorders and maladjustment may also qualify. Severe misbehavior can lead to a court martial and even prison, so don't try too hard.

Jury Duty

What is jury duty? How does it work?
Every English-speaking U.S. citizen 18 or older has the right and obligation to serve as a juror when called to do so in a criminal or civil trial. An accused has the right to a trial by a jury of his peers, and that may mean you.

Do I have to serve?
Yes. If you don't appear you may be held in contempt, and you may have to pay a fine.

Do I get paid for it?
You may receive a nominal pay from the courts. In some states, employers are also required to pay employees their salary up to a certain limit while serving on jury duty. A person can't be fired or discriminated against because he or she has to serve on jury duty.

What are some of the acceptable excuses?
- Severe medical or financial hardship
- Age of 75 or older
- Being the main caregiver for an ill or handicapped person
- Emergency health care providers such as firefighters

What are my rights and obligations as a juror?
You may choose between:
- A) Listen to the judge's instructions and follow them to the letter, hear the prosecutor's and the defense attorney's case. Then, along with the other jurors, try to arrive at an unanimous decision avoiding a "hung jury", which may lead to another trial.

B) Be a more active juror. Use the judge's instructions as guidelines only. Familiarize yourself with a juror's rights, including the power to reduce the charges against a defendant. Beware of multiple charges brought by a prosecutor in the hopes that at least one of the accusations will "stick". If you feel that a law is unjust or does not apply to the accused, you can vote with your conscience without the fear you will be punished for it. You may inform and instruct the other juror's of their rights but do not bring any pamphlets or brochures about the subject to court. Finally, remember that a "hung jury" may sometimes be the best option.

Guns

What are the rules regarding concealed weapons?
States that prohibit concealed weapons:
- Kansas
- Missouri
- Nebraska
- New Mexico
- Ohio
- Wisconsin

States that allow concealed weapons for applicants who demonstrate a specific need for it, such as a security guard or a person who regularly carries large amounts of cash.
- Alabama
- California
- Colorado
- Connecticut
- Delaware
- Hawaii
- Iowa
- Maryland
- Massachusetts
- Michigan
- Minnesota
- New Jersey
- New York
- Rhode Island

Vermont is the only state that does not require a license for carrying concealed weapons. All other 28 states require some kind of a permit for concealed weapons but no specific reason from the applicant is needed.

What are the restrictions for gun ownership?

You must be 18 or older to purchase or own a shotgun or rifle and at least 21 for other legal firearms. Certain individuals are barred from gun ownership. Excluded are those with a history of drug and heavy alcohol use, felons, illegal aliens, and people who are mentally incompetent. It also applies to persons convicted of a domestic violence or who have a restraining order related to it.

Is it legal to buy a gun from a private individual?

Yes it is. But what guarantee do you have that the gun has not been stolen or used to commit a crime? If you do purchase a gun from a private individual or at a flea market, make sure to register it.

Legitimate firearms dealers or sporting goods stores carry the appropriate paperwork that will ensure you are legally qualified to purchase and own a gun.

What if the cops find a gun in my car?

If a handgun is found in your vehicle, it is yours until proven otherwise. Without a permit, you may be charged and arrested, even if somebody else claims ownership of the gun.

Voting

How do I register to vote?

You can register to vote while applying for a driver's license, or in many high schools, libraries, or at the post office. You can even register to vote on-line using the Internet.

Do I have to vote?

No. Neither voting nor voting registration are an obligation in the U.S. As opposed to many other nations, you will not be fined and your rights will not diminish if you don't vote. The sad truth is that most young Americans don't exercise their right to vote, especially at the local community level, even though a single alderman's decision may influence your life more than a president's four year term.

What if I am out of town?

You have the option of pre-voting in your own district, before the actual elections. As an alternative for out of town voters, you can opt to mail your ballot to the jurisdiction where you belong. In either case, a special envelope signed by the voter has to be utilized for the ballot, and the vote is not counted until regular votes have been tallied.

CHAPTER THIRTEEN

Computers, the Internet, and You

"I think there is a world market for maybe five computers."
- Thomas Watson, Chairman of IBM, 1943

In the early days of television, some people felt uneasy changing clothes in front of the TV for fear that they could be seen by the person who, so easily, could reach the privacy of their homes through the airwaves. Ludicrous, you say?

Now, fifty years later, comes the computer (and the Internet), and many users don't give a second thought about exposing themselves through it. If "Big Brother" were to design a malicious plot to spy on citizens, on their tastes, habits, political interests, sexual preferences, and literally everything else, they could not come up with a better plan than the computer-Internet symbiosis. Instead of secretly installing microphones and cameras in each home, an intelligent being could make a device so attractive and useful that everyone would want it, willingly bringing it home, and even paying for the privilege of owning it.

In our society, the use of computers is so pervasive that we don't notice it anymore. The cable box on top of the TV is a computer that may inform the cable company of your viewing habits, or the movies you prefer, and whether you were changing channels at two in the morning. Another example is the credit card reader at your local 7-Eleven. It will record not only the "Slurpie" you bought, but will also stamp the date and the location where you bought it, effectively tracking you and your spending habits. Even your computerized hospital records are as safe as the next disgruntled employee, same as your job history and the money you owe the IRS.

On the good side, this same easy access to information is probably the most democratizing development since the invention of Gutenberg's printing press. Anyone with a computer can communicate and exchange ideas with everybody else on the planet, instantaneously and without geographical boundaries. There is no limit to the range of subjects available for research or discussion: gossip, news, music, pornography, art, and a million others.

Some say the Internet is too open. Should there be a limit? Who should be responsible for the daunting task of setting the guidelines, the laws for what is proper or not? For example, what is obscene? Certainly not Michelangelo's naked statue of David. Then, what about Mapplethorpe's *really* disturbing erotic photos? Can the picture of a nude starving boy in Africa, or your baby photos in the bathtub be considered "kiddie porn"? Our legal system is ill prepared to deal with technology's accelerating rate of change, and the upcoming Internet laws are likely to become obsolete faster than the computers they were written on.

Is my home e-mail private?

E-mail is at least as private as the regular post office mail you receive. However, under certain circumstances, both your regular correspondence and the e-mail you send or receive may be legally "opened" by a government agency. Sending threatening e-mails to someone gives the authorities probable cause, and it is a surefire way to get your future e-mails screened. Penalties for threatening e-mails vary depending on the perceived seriousness of its contents. For example, an otherwise innocent e-mail message from a teenager to a colleague, venting frustration over being bullied in school, but mentioning the word "kill" in its contents, could be construed as a threat.

Can my boss go through my computer files?

There is no privacy when it comes to your office computer, including e-mail. The employer has the right to oversee all the work you do while performing your job, even without your knowledge. The private romantic letter you wrote to your girlfriend, or the racist joke somebody e-mailed you are fair game. Depending on the file contents, it can get you reprimanded or even fired. The e-mails on your computer may haunt you even years after they were exchanged. Some companies may go as far as to attach a device to the keyboard of "problem employees" that records every keystroke they make, for later retrieval, even if the text is not actually saved to the computer memory.

Who owns the private work that I created on the office computer, after my regular work hours?

Unless there is a private agreement, all the work done on the company's computer and other equipment belongs to them. The same is also true if you use an employer's bench lab or the company's lathe to develop a new invention. The universities are no exception and even though you may become famous for publishing an original work, you may not reap any financial benefits from it unless previously agreed by both parties. The situation becomes even more complicated if you begin your research at one place of employment and you are hired by another private business or school to continue it.

Do the police need a warrant to search my personal computer?
Yes. If probable cause exists, a warrant may be issued and a computer can be physically removed from your home or business, and thoroughly searched. If any illegal activity is found on your files, it may be used against you, even if the evidence found is not directly related to the original charges that led to the warrant.

Is it true that a computer keeps information even if it has been deleted?
Deleting a file does not erase it from the computer's memory; it just puts it in a trashcan. Even after you empty the computer trashcan, the files remain accessible to resourceful individuals. One can rummage through the deleted files and, most of the time, it is still possible to read them.

Before you decide to sell or give your old computer away, remember that your private information remains in the computer's hard drive. You will need special software to write random data over the deleted files, effectively erasing the magnetic imprint from the disk. Also, remove the floppy disk, CD or any other storage medium you may have forgotten in the computer, before you part with it. Unscrupulous people have been known to purchase old computers at garage sales or business just for the information contained in them.

Does the computer remember where I have "surfed" on the Internet?
Unless you adjust your software to do otherwise, each time you visit a website, it will attach a tag, known as a "cookie", to the surfing you do with the computer. A "cookie" is identified by a unique number that recognizes and follows the computer wherever it travels on the Internet, while, at the same time, allowing the computer itself to remain anonymous. For example, a weather forecast site may display ads or "banners" advertising an allergy medication. Clicking on one of those banners will redirect you to the allergy website, which will read the "cookie", and immediately identify the new visitor as originating from the weather page.

The computer also keeps a log of the sites visited on a file named "History", which contains the dates and times each website was accessed. Deleting the file does not erase it (see above).

Is it legal to download music and video for my own use off the Net?

Everybody does it, but it is still illegal. It does infringe on the copyright of the artist that developed the product, and the company that produced it, who are both legally and morally entitled to sell it to the public. Music sales are down, possibly as a direct consequence of the widespread availability of free music to be downloaded.

Is it legal to download pornographic material off the Net?

Pornography is among the biggest moneymakers on the Net. The legal loophole to distribute and download sexual content on the Internet is that pornography is very tricky to define, and therefore difficult to prosecute. The exception comes when pornography involves underage subjects who, legally, cannot consent to sex.

The so called "kiddie porn" is not a legal gray area, and possession of this type of material is usually prosecuted to the full extent of the law. Juries and judges are likely to be revolted by the sexual exploitation of children and even a good attorney will have a hard time getting a pedophile off the hook. Stay away from websites or any printed material that displays underage pornography, even if you are underage yourself.

Is it safe to use my credit card on the computer?

With proper precautions, yes. Make sure that any personal information you send is done so through a secure server. This is done by verifying that the website in question uses safety measures, such as encryption, to keep someone from eavesdropping on the information you submit.

In real life, you are more likely to have your credit card number stolen by a dishonest employee who works at a gas station or at a department store, than by making a purchase over the Internet.

110

Resources

Brain, Marshall. <u>The Teenager's Guide to the Real World</u>. Raleigh, NC: BYG Publishing, 1997.

Courtwright, David T. <u>Forces of Nature: Drugs and the Making of the Modern World.</u> Cambridge: Harvard University Press, 2001.

Everett, Jack W. <u>The Truth about Trusts, A Trustee's Survival Guide</u>. FTPC Publishing, 1999.

Garner, Bryan A., ed. <u>Black's Law Dictionary</u> . 2nd ed. West Information Pub Group, 2001.

Loewy, Arnold H. <u>Criminal Law in a Nutshell</u>. 3rd ed. West Information Pub Group, 1999.

<u>The New Lawyer's Wit and Wisdom; Quotations of the Legal Profession, in Brief</u>. Ed. Bruce Nash and Allen Zullo. Philadelphia: Running Press, 1995.

Pressman, David. <u>Patent it Yourself</u>. 9th ed. Nolo Press, 2002.

Wallace, L. Jean. <u>What Every 18-Year Old Needs to Know about Texas Law</u>. Austin: University of Texas Press, 1997.

Wallace, Richard, II. <u>An Educated Guide to Speeding Tickets: How to Beat and Avoid Them</u>. Worchester, MA: "T-Bird" Books. 1996.

Online Sources

Emory University: School of Law. 15 June 2002. <http://www.law.emory.edu/erd/index.html>

Find Law- Law, Lawyers, and Legal Resources. 15 June 2002. <http://www.findlaw.com>.

Law. Net. 15 June 2002. <http://www.law.net/>.

National Consumer Law Center. 15 June 2002. <http://www.consumerlaw.org/frames/main.htm>.

Nolo: Law for All. 15 June 2002. <http://www.nolo.com>.

The New York Times: College. 15 June 2002. <http://www.nytimes.com/college/index.html>.

INDEX

Arbitration 61, 62
Arraignment 26, 27
Arrest 10, 13, 16, 17, 26, 27, 28, 29, 34
Automobile accidents 23

Bail 27
Bankruptcy 46, 47
Blood alcohol level 19, 20
Blood samples 32
Breathalyzer 5, 20, 21
Bribery 15

Civil suit 28, 30
Community service 29
Consumer Credit Counseling Service 46
Contract 49, 50, 51, 52, 64, 68
Criminal suit 30

DMV 15, 24
DUI 17, 19, 20, 21, 22

Entrapment 37
Executor 58

Fake ID 34
Felony 26, 28, 29, 35, 36, 37, 38, 41, 56
Fines 29, 34, 56

Grand jury 27

Hazing 56

Impounded 12
Indecent exposure 41
Indictment 27
Insurance 5

Landlord 53
Laser 18
Litigation 30, 61
Living will 59

Marijuana 26, 29, 32, 36, 37, 38
Mediation 61, 62, 64
Miranda Law 13
Misdemeanor 26, 28, 29, 34, 56
Moving violations 7, 17

No contest 16, 28
Non-moving violations 17

Open alcohol containers 21
Out-of-state fine 16

Plea bargain 25, 27
Point system 15
Points 7, 15, 16, 36, 44
Preliminary hearing 27
Premiums 5, 15, 16, 23
Probate 58, 59
Probation 28, 29, 31, 34, 38, 56, 68
Public intoxication 35
Pulled over 5, 9, 10, 12

Radar 18
Rape 39, 40
Resisting arrest 13
Restitution 29, 63, 70

Searches 12, 56
Security deposit 51
Sexual harassment 40, 66
Small claims court 61, 62
Speedometer 18

Statutory rape 40
Streaking 41

Three strike law 29
Ticket 8, 9, 10, 15, 16, 17, 18, 26
Traffic school 16
Traffic violations 7
Trust 59

Urine drug screen 31

Warrant 12, 16, 17
Will 58
Worker's compensation 69

Acknowledgements

We would like to thank Officer Daniel Parris from the Memphis Police Department for his invaluable tips and candid advice when we began writing this book.

Our gratitude for the teachings and corrections suggested by Honorable J.D. Alissandratos, and for his contagious affection for all things legal.

Finally, a special thanks to Mrs. Nancy Johnson, our first grade teacher. She must have done something right.